ELEVEN FOURTHS

SALLY SMITH

AuthorHouse™
1663 Liberty Drive
Bloomington, IN 47403
www.authorhouse.com
Phone: 1 (800) 839-8640

Published by AuthorHouse   02/27/2018

ISBN: 978-1-5462-2380-1 (sc)
ISBN: 978-1-5462-2381-8 (e)

Print information available on the last page.

This book is printed on acid-free paper.

authorHOUSE®

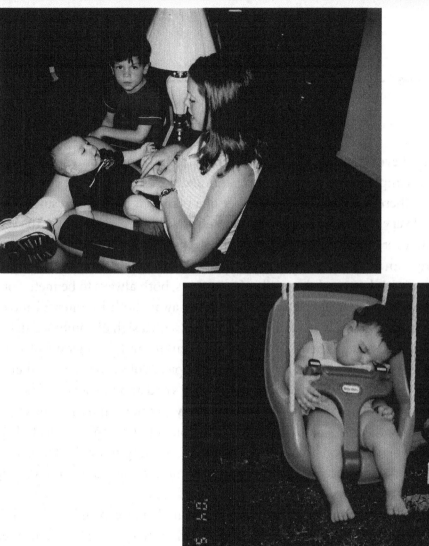

In the start of every day, usually only separated from the one before it by a few hours of sleep, lies unparalleled insanity in repetition of tasks fought to be completed, and battles to be waged. There is always one small fiber of a plan that unravels, resulting in total disaster on my end. Every piece of information and understanding, gathered over the years, so carefully placed with energy and time invested in the darkness, gets covered with the picture missed. Daily there is an email to be sent, a question to be answered, and a call to be made. There are my battles for his best, and the needs of my others, both always to be met. For every piece of the puzzle laid, two get ripped apart and blown away, both by internal forces and external actions of others. Most days end just as they start, with a sigh of combined defeat and frustration, culminating in that moment of the last system failure and the opening of a pressure relief valve. Every day I get a little closer, to putting all the pieces of his puzzle together. Every day there is a tiny space of time suspended between one day's end and the next day's start. This tiny space is the stopping point for these arms that can't carry anymore, and the hands that must release the clenched fists; there is a mutually embraced moment of complete defeat, disguised as fleeting peace and resignation on both our parts. I want nothing more than to just exhale, alone, in the moment of acceptance of all I cannot do, no matter how many hours I fought to accomplish the task.

In this moment, Oren has finally struggled through all that he can and realizes the day is done; in his peace, still he has unrest. In these moments where he is drawn like a magnet back to me, I gain some of my most profound insight into my child's mind. I am, at best, similar to a mad scientist, and at worst, my own experiment. I learn instantly from my mistakes – usually a quick reaction verbally or physically from Oren, to a totally unintentionally irritating act on my part. It was in my demand that he stop moving his feet on me, that we talked about his legs feeling like they wiggle endlessly inside; and in order to stop this sensation, he wiggles them. When I placed my legs on his in order to prove to him that the weight of his legs could be irritating, I saw his eyes roll back indicating his "input" button was pressed just right.

It was in my tearful demand that he stop staring at me, as he watched TV through me, that I realized I am his gauge on reality in its entirety and that very few other people, does he watch. Oren watches me while we watch T.V., usually a how to program such as cooking or home renovation, and usually a movie that we have seen a thousand times, as he takes great comfort in the repetition. Together, in that small wrinkle of time, as we forget the horrendous ordeals of the day, there are great truths. This is why he sits sideways, placed not as to see the TV straight on, but so he can keep me in his line of vision along with the TV. If I laugh he knows that what he heard immediately before that, must be funny, and if I make a sound indicating sadness, he attempts to store logical empathy.

It is my belief that with repetition of the same movie, Oren learns to put these pieces together and gain social understanding. In yet another moment of learning, I discovered that Oren, at times, has visual fields similar the way a fly sees, and avoids looking at people's faces because the images of a thousand eyes are too much to bear. In watching Oren wrap himself up in a blanket like a mummy, was the determination made that he needed a body sock for compression. In realizing he only feels emotions as an "empty" feeling, was I able to understand his endless hunger was his way of communicating being sad or mad. These moments create incredible growth in understanding, yet have very real potential for harm. Without these moments and the ability for me to see how my actions must be viewed on his side of the fishbowl, I would not be able to help those around him understand his behaviors.

I am missing so many pieces to his puzzle, and every one that is dislodged by those around us while they shove their own incorrect version of clarity into our world that doesn't fit in the picture, makes us work harder to get our life picture perfect. Had I not been in the moment with Oren when his literal interpretation of a recipe altered the amount of water from 1 1/4cups to 11/4 (eleven fourths) and reacted quickly; had I not suffered his anguish and thrown random ingredients like root beer and flour and sugar into his red soup meant to be red velvet cake batter, determined to make his effort worthwhile, as he threw his body into walls and created destruction all around us at his intolerance to own mistakes, this whole process would not have started. Eleven fourths. Autism does not see the way the rest of the world does.

It is my belief that my child sees everything as a picture snapshot. When the picture he has created in his head is mismatched against reality, he simply cannot understand or process it. Every child's picture is different and ever changing, with each moment processed on an entirely different plane than the rest of the world. This story was written to help those around us, who should exist to help my child navigate through his world, and yet so many times create more chaos and destruction around us, with their "interventions" and own closed-minded beliefs. Most often, those in place to help our cause engage in discriminatory judgment of my child and our family, without the tools necessary to take that task on. In some instances, this resulted in simple misunderstandings, in others, real harm to my child and our family. Oren's story is sad and brilliant, as told in his own words, if he could share it verbally. I am hopeful his story will remind us all to advocate and empathize in order to get their child's needs met.

Each child, whether special or with special needs, was placed in the care of hands, chosen by a higher power that knows best.

Those around will never quite understand, whether stranger or family, why we fight for our children. Most will maintain only an obstructive force. As the parent, we have the opportunity to listen and watch, and wear the hat of empathy to solve the mystery of our child's needs. Never, ever give up.

Everyone keeps coming to my house, making my mom spend time talking to them. I can hear her telling them about me, so that they can help us. Sometimes the things they talk about are the bad things I do that I think about, but I can't stop doing. I wrote my mom a note yesterday, and tried to say thank you for fighting for me, but by the time she got it she didn't want to read it because I had already fought with her for three hours. I have ideas about things I want to eat and do and where to go and what I want other people to do, all day long. If I can't make those things happen just like the picture in my head, I can't seem to do anything at all. Even if we are going to do something fun, I can't add anything to my picture or it gets all messed up. I don't mean to do things; sometimes it makes me even more angry when I try to stop getting those things I want. I do try sometimes because I can see my mom's face every once in a while, and she doesn't smile anymore. I know that a smile means happy. And I know when my belly feels full and good and warm and my face makes that shape like the smile I see on other people's faces I'm not thinking about the next thing I want to do. Maybe that is what it means for me to be happy.

My name is Oren, and instead of everybody trying to get my mom to tell our story, or see if the story she tells makes sense to them, maybe everybody that keeps coming to our house should help my mom take care of me and my brothers. Maybe you could hear and see the reasons for her being mad, instead of trying to say there's no excuse for her anger. She's been fighting for me and with me for a long time now, and our story used to be spoken softly until no one would listen. Now my mom yells a lot, and her face doesn't make that shape of a smile, and I want my mom back. She's not trying to tell her own story, that's not why people are coming to our house and making it dirty with their germs, and taking her time away from us. She yells because you can't hear her, and you are missing what she's trying to tell you, which is my story.

My mom keeps fighting to get my story heard. Now more people want to come, and I'm still not going anywhere after school, or on the weekend to get out of here for a break. Sometimes I look at the fish inside the glass box and I see my face in the same glass; I look at people like that too so the picture makes sense to me. But my mom and brothers don't like to look out from the water side of the glass, or people staring at them from the side without water.

Why are more people coming all the time that I don't know – their faces are funny and their smell is funny and when they sit on the sofa they don't match the picture in my head of what our family room looks like. They say they are going to help, but all they do is make my mom talk and talk and talk, when I want to be with her. I don't like to keep hearing stories about myself and the things that I do. I can't stop trying to get the picture in my head to match this side of my glass bowl, no matter how much I hurt the people around me. My baby brother hears me when I say, "I'm hungry, I'm hungry", and he tells my mom to give him one of what he is eating so he can give it to me. He doesn't understand that I'm not really hungry, I just only feel that one thing if I am upset, which is me thinking my belly is empty. My baby brother helps me come inside when my mom tells me its time but I get mad and start to fight with her. Kushie says "come on 'Owen' time to go in" (he can't say my name right because he's too little) and he takes my hand and helps me go. I can remember sometimes that I have to do what he says because I'm the big brother, even though Kushie acts like the big brother to me. Sometimes I get so mad there's no way to stop, even though I don't want to hurt anybody, especially Kush. My mom knows that and that's why she keeps trying to have me live at home, even though no one else around us thinks she should. But my mom's face looks more tired and "not happy" every day. That's what little Kushie says "I not happy". I wish I could tell everybody how I felt like my little brother does, then maybe I wouldn't be so mad. Even though I hurt my family sometimes, they still help me. He will pick out my favorite chips at the store and give them to my mom and say, "here mama, these are 'hot chee-os' for 'Owen'" and his own face gets really "lighted up" when he tells me he brought them from the store for me. My mom reminds me when he does all these things how much he loves me and how important it is that I stop doing all these bad things in front of him.

I feel my face crumple up sometimes; I want to rip my own arms off because I'm so mad at the me inside the fish bowl when I want something so bad I can't stop. My hands hurt my family and even though I see their faces get really dark or what my mom says sadness looks like, I can't stop hurting them. I used to bang my head on the wall as hard as I could to try to knock the picture in my head out so I could stop being mad. My mom got me a trampoline that I jump on when the pictures in my head don't match the picture my body is in; sometimes if I jump as soon as the pictures change, I can shake the images around enough and get back off the trampoline and not be angry. When Kushie got bigger he wanted to jump too, but to play. If he gets in my way when I need to jump to "picture change", I get mad at him. If my mom can see my picture changing soon enough, she can help Kushie to rock in the rocking chair and I can still jump, or she helps us both rock together.

I've broken out 5 glass windows with my hands, and only stopped when I saw the blood running down my arm; that was the last time we lived in an upstairs house because my mom was so scared I might fall out. My mom had a special window made with glass that couldn't cut me before we moved to our next house. Please help my mom stay in our house, because I can't get my story out or what I need without my mom, but I can't stay here and keeping hurting my family either. You can't keep coming and making my mom tell you my story and changing my pictures and then leaving without doing anything about it, or maybe you shouldn't come at all. I need my mom for as long as I can have her, because she's the only one that can tell when my pictures don't matchup. She's the only one that helps me figure out what I need to have done.

My mom knows how to figure out why I stand so close to the TV when the doctor tells her my eyes are okay; why I can't hear when my hearing test are normal and why I can only eat certain things because only a few foods taste the way the pictures tell me they should. Every fight for me she has to take on, takes her away from me and makes her face darker and sadder. My mom is the only one that ever asked me what the picture in my head looks like, or gave me ear plugs to help me hear, or showed me how a fly can see like me. My mom can hear the words in my head and she takes them and puts them in her mouth to tell you what I can't. My mom and Will, my big brother, aren't like Kushie. He loves me without being mad at what I do – so far – like my mom used to be. But after I started hurting my family, that changed, and she says she can't let one child hurt another one of her children. With my mom's help, I will tell you my story, from baby until now, the best I can remember. Later, if you forget what me and my mom and my brothers look like on the "water side" of the glass bowl, you can read it again and my mom can read me a story instead of fight with any of you, because she can't keep fighting with me and for me, against everyone else.

My mom starting fighting for me a long time ago. Parts of my story I think my big brother Will may have told me but I have seen pictures that match the picture in my head when I hear stories about me. I used to like to look through the pictures of all of us, but now I look away because everybody's smile is broken in the pictures of me when I am older. Kush shows our mom pictures of a year ago, and I hear him tell her "mama is happy…'wook' Mama, happy wit Kushie".

When my mom and me and Will first moved to this city, my mom used to help me in the pool at the apartment complex we lived in. I wasn't as scared of water then, and I used to hold onto her back and we would swim all the way down to the bottom of the pool together and I was not afraid. The world would go quiet inside the fishbowl with my mom and I did not see any glass or any sides. We would climb to the top of the huge hill with the giant pirate ship on top (I found out later it was actually the big satellite towers on top of the hill) but my mom always called it the pirate ship. I never could go very far, because my bones and muscles just couldn't do it and I'd get too tired, so my mom would put me on a big rock and I would climb on top of her back and she would carry me all the way up to the big ship.

We started walking before we moved to the big city, when we first moved to this state after my mom and dad got divorced. I was only two then, so I don't know about all that, but I know I was little and I know my mom would smile at me as I ran, and when she tells the story of the pictures, she said I ran with a broken chicken wing, my arm tucked up under itself as I swung the other one so hard to get going. We went to the park all the times, after I could walk, and I like to look at the pictures of me and my mom and big brother on the slides and playing all the time. Somewhere in my mind I remember my mom sitting or lying at my side for hour after hour every night before I turned three while I screamed like I was being tortured, until finally falling asleep. In the world of darkness and screams my mom couldn't reach it and couldn't get me out, so she just stayed at my side through it. Besides, there wasn't anybody else to take a turn with me. There's never anybody that takes a turn that doesn't take something else from us and I think that's why my mom doesn't let anyone pretend to do it anymore.

When I finally did say a few words (not really talking yet) I said "wa-ter" with a Caribbean accent at the same time I put my hand to my mouth and cheek to say water silently to my mom as we came down a hill and saw a tiny waterfall. I was past three years old then. My mom had taught me sign language as soon as it was clear I wasn't going to speak on time or maybe even ever. There was this one woman that would come and do therapy or "play" at the house every week, but when I turned three she stopped coming. But my mom kept playing steam roller with me, and always made sure I had a backpack with soup cans in it to help me not feel like I was coming apart and floating away. She gave me another one at the end of last school year, when no one would weigh me down with anything out of the magazines with cool tools for kids like me, because it cost too much. That's when a friend showed my mom how to make weighted blankets and made one for me.

When I was a baby, my mom learned a lot about what to do for me because she had people around that wanted to help her help me. So, they taught her what to do, like my therapy and infant massage that she did every night after my bath and that I hated, along with my physical therapy so that I would be able to sit up by myself. I had to wear a helmet for along time that in pictures looks bigger than me, because I would not stop banging my head on the wall, and the floor, and even other people until I would get bruises all over my head.

When I got the shots every day to stop my seizures, my brother tells me how my mom got very worried about my immune system. She made everyone wash their hands a thousand times, and even the man with the hose to kill the bugs had to put on shoe covers; she even sprayed the conveyer belt at the grocery story with disinfectant spray before she put the food on it. And she wouldn't let anyone touch me except for my family. We had to go in the car a lot to see the doctors out of town, but I also had to do my therapy every week and my mom had to work extra because of all the bills, so she worked 4 days a week at the hospital and every Friday for the pediatrician that finally diagnosed me back when I was 9 months old.

I don't think she's had time off since I was born except for when Kushie was born… it was a hard schedule to keep for my mom so she took a travel job out of town and we were all going to move there, my dad too, in December of that year. My mom would come home every time she could to see us. But I think my dad had a few friends over and must have made a mess or something that made mom mad. I guess Will saw one of my dad's friends and her daughter at daycare and told my mom that she came over to play with him while my mom was gone working. My mom left again, but this time I went with her.

She drove with me all alone to the town she was working in, with the back doors of our car duct taped because there were no child locks and I tried to open the door while she was on the highway (still have that bad habit). But we made it and soon after she found a safe place for me to stay while she worked her shifts, and a spot opened for Will and he came too. There was a whole lot of things to do outside and there were lots of hills and great winding roads to go fast on, and this would help move me so fast that I felt so still and calm. There weren't many people that needed new friends, or that me and Will and my mom could count on. My mom had made one friend, a best friend, while she was working there and alone, that made us two great blankets and had taken my mom on the windiest road ever, and she got her best friend to help take us to see it too. This friend helped my mom not be so afraid. She had walked my mom right up to the edge of the Grand Canyon with a blindfold on and held her safe so that the first time my mom ever saw it, she was standing on the edge of the world. So, my mom took us to the same spot so we could see the same thing she did…anything my mom learned or got to do she would show us, and teach me about it.

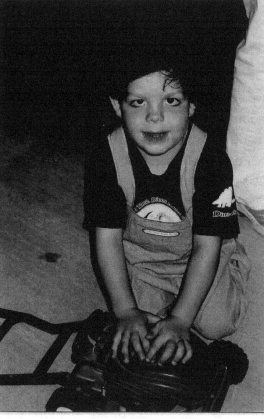

We used to chase trains every time we went back to visit Will before he could live with us. I love trains. And tools. And sports cars. When tools disappear now I can feel my mom look at me first. My mom knows a lot about a lot of things, when she tells me something about things we pass by when we go for rides, I remember. If I get the chance to see what we saw again, it's always exactly like she explained to me. Every time I see an airplane (or rocket ship, that's what Kushie calls them), especially at night, I watch to see how many are lined up, top to bottom and I look side to side to watch as the ones that are waiting to get in line turn and take their own spot. I never looked up and around like that until my mom showed me. She said, "think about all the things going on all around you that you could miss if you never looked up". My mom seems to know that even if I don't get it right then, the words she says will roll around in my head until they hit the right spots and all of a sudden, the pictures line up, and I understand.

There has only been one time my mom didn't know what to do. I hear my mom say all the time that if she knows something, she knows it better than many, and if she doesn't, she'll be the first to admit it and call for help. And when she didn't know what to do, she called for that help. It was after hours of trying to help me get my picture right in my head (but before she knew exactly about which pictures weren't matching) but I didn't have a picture in my head and something else was wrong somewhere else.

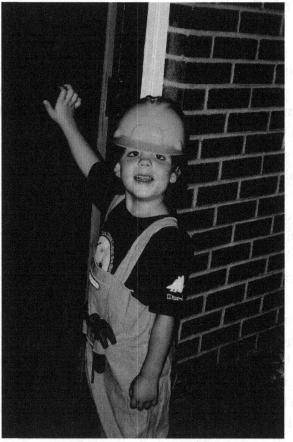

Usually I feel it in my belly, and that's why I always say I'm hungry when I'm not. I don't feel emotions like my mom or my brothers do, especially now. My mom asked me a few days ago if I could love and what that meant to me and felt like. She always asks me questions like that when we go for rides together and kushie falls asleep and she turns the music down really low. I can hear her because she makes her questions match the sound of the music and the words make sense to me. If she asks me questions about something that happened, she knows now that I have to have time to get all the pictures lined up right. Every moment has the picture in my head and the memory of what really happened and I have to pick out the truth. She waits sometimes for minutes and sometimes for days, and sometimes we both just forget. But this wasn't that kind of question and I could answer during that same ride in the truck. I told her that if I thought of loving somebody it made me want to not be mean and act nice or do something for them and try hard not to get upset when the picture changed. I told her that "not anymore do I feel love for anyone. I think she already knew the one time I felt that way and why I can't anymore.

See, the one time my mom called for help was very late at night, actually all the way into the next day at 2:00 in the morning. She had called at midnight earlier, but thought she could help me herself since the crisis people were going to take about 2 hours to get there and they weren't the team that knew me. The only part of my mom that is broken I think is her arms. It seems hard for her to get them around me and my brother sometimes; maybe that's because she's put them out so much and not gotten any arms back that she quit trying. But that night, because the part of me that was broken had never even been used before, we didn't know it could break. So, she didn't know how to help me fix a broken heart because she didn't know what that looked like for me.

I heard her tell the story when the people came, about what had happened a few days ago with one of the caregivers at my after-school program. This was when I tried to jump out of the van when we were going really fast on the highway, after he said what he said to me. His face went dark and his eyes had no light in them. I heard her tell them that she watched "my soul shatter" and my whole body crumple to the floor like my face crumples when I am upset, and like I lost all my shape. She said it was like I couldn't hold up my own body anymore. And she was right. I had leaned on the door but it didn't help keep me standing up. I had put my hands over my face and heard myself making the same sound my mom makes from behind her bedroom door when she thought we were all asleep at night. My hands got wet and my mouth tasted like salt I felt so heavy and the pain I get in my belly was up higher in my chest and up my throat. There was a hole being made there, right where I used to feel the vibrations I felt for the first time because of how I felt attached to this caregiver, and thought he was my friend. And my mom couldn't make her arms work right, so she called for help for my broken heart.

My mom keeps telling my story, even as it changes and things get added, bad things keep coming and my mom keeps telling and nobody hears her. After all the bad that happened at my after-school program, nobody cared about my words or story, when they came out in the sound of her voice. My mom gave my teacher a tape recorder to put in my pocket at the end of the school day before I went to the after-school program. She knew something was wrong, and that I couldn't tell her, and maybe when I finally lined up the pictures in the right order it would be too late. So, she decided to get my truth without my pictures and only with the sounds around me.

At first, I remembered the recorder was in my pocket, but when it got too noisy at the program I forgot all about that…until I had to remember because it flew out of my pocket when I got shoved onto my knees and my belly and my face was shoved into the ground. This happened after he dragged me out from under the table where I was hiding. He pulled me across the floor and into another room, where I was alone with him. I usually move slow but I moved fast then so the person hurting me couldn't see the recorder. I got it back in my pocket somehow before I forgot about it again. My leg and back hurt so bad being twisted and bent like that I couldn't think of anything else but making that pain stop.

I saw the shoes of the kids and the other caregivers in the class walk by me in the other room where I was trapped and alone. He kept me there and told me over and over when I stopped crying he would let me go, but I couldn't stop crying because my leg hurt so bad. All I wanted was my mom…where was she? I finally changed the picture in my head so that the pain went to a different Oren and I could stop crying long enough for him to take me to the other room. He shoved me down again and I had to stay there with my hurt leg while he sat in a chair higher up than me and stared at me. I watched the clock on the wall and knew they had to let me go home soon. A few minutes before we were to get on the vans to go home I was still crying and angry, and the room was still too loud, but I was too afraid to fight back any more because I didn't want my leg and back to feel like that again. And everybody else was too afraid to tell that man to stop hurting me because he would hurt them too. As the minutes passed, I got calmer because I knew I could get home.

That was the last night I ever had to go to the program or ride on the van. When I got to my house, my mom and one of the new behavioral support people were there waiting. My mom asked me to give her the recorder and I did and then went to take my bath and my medications. The next day my mom called this program and the biggest fight of her life up to that point started. I guess that man thought my mom would be to scared of him to go there. To make sure he went out front and stood and stared at her when she went to get the paper with the lies on it that told a story different than the one on the recorder did. But my mom still walked by him to get that paper and since she only sees one face when she looks at people she looked right into his eyes. I heard her tell somebody later when telling the story of that moment, that she would have emptied the whole paperclip into him, if she needed to, but that didn't really make sense to me. She called everybody she was supposed to – the police, the owner of the program, the people that come for all the meetings all the times, and their bosses and bosses boss. Then things got really far away from the picture and the sounds of that day, and somebody came and scared my mom so she stopped talking about what happened to me. But I know she knows what happened because she never made me go back there once she heard the picture I couldn't say with my words.

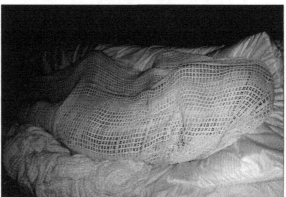

When I was smaller, like Kushie, my mom used to shake her head quietly when she discovered some of the things I had done, like unscrewing all the hinges or doorknobs on a door quickly and quietly. Nobody would know until they grabbed a door and it fell off from all but the top area. When my collections of rocks grew from small hills to mountains and she found pebbles all across the house in a trail leading to where I had them hidden under my bed.

All these years my mom would laugh as I changed and grew and learned, but now when my mom laughs I go really fast to see what made that noise because I don't hear it very often. When my mom plays the piano, I go very fast to her side and stand quietly to hear the sound, because I don't hear it very often. My mom doesn't need your help to understand me, or tell her what does or doesn't work. My mom can tell you about the picture in my head that has to stay the same or my whole world falls apart. My mom can tell you what I need even when I don't know. My mom knows my truth.

I am more than my diagnoses of Kabuki syndrome and Autism. I can and will do more than the doctors told my mom when I was a baby and diagnosed with infantile spasms. I was never to walk, talk, or tie my own shoes. I am more than the bad things I do. When I laugh from my belly, it makes others laugh too. I have dreams of living in my own little house on a farm with my mom when I'm grown up. I think I want to work on electronics and fix things, not always break them. I love to watch football, even though I can't play it. I love the numbers and the stats of all my favorite players. If I can live how I need to, in a body sock under a weight blanket, and people that are to help me, actually help me, not hurt me, I can be the best version of me I was meant to be.

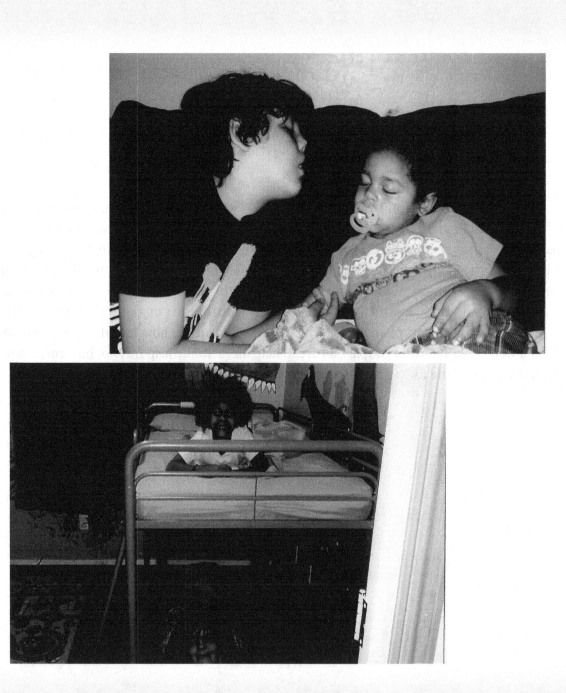

Acknowledgements

O ren is in high school now, and meets new challenges every day, on his journey to self-advocacy and independence. The fight continues, with the only change being the players. We don't know why the people that have caused harm, have. I know I have seen horrible acts toward my child, and phenomenal acts of empathy and humanity from those that surround us on our path. To those that touched us, consider your actions forever immortalized in the following words:

For Misty Pando, for acknowledging a mother's intuition that something was wrong with Oren and pushing me to challenge his current pediatrician, for driving to the hospital hours away, and all the road trips to doctors that followed.

For Theresa Hendley, who was a dear friend and mentor and who allowed me to adjust my schedule to meet work and home needs during Oren's illness.

For Beth Parks, who walked me to the edge and taught me not to be afraid.

For Vicki Steele, who made and designed the first weight blanket for Oren and taught me to sew so that I can help others.

For CFSS, for all their support, and the resources and phenomenal people we were given the opportunity to work with.

For Debbie Miera, and her insight into Oren's mind and her sensory intelligence

For Linda Aufrance, whose friendship and unending support I am eternally grateful for, and whose sewing-machine I still have.

For Heather Solky, whose years of dedication and hard work as Oren's elementary and middle school teacher, challenged and encouraged Oren's academic and social growth.

For Miss Kris and Miss Shelly, who watched out for Oren at school all these years.

For Earl LeBlanc, who helped without return in those early years and whose words of wisdom I still hear in my mind

For Anna Marie Prieto, who, from Kush's birth, when she held my puke bucket, until today, jumps in and helps no matter what.

For my parents, Tom and Vicki Goff, a.k.a "Ya-Ya" and "Poppa", who gave me my fight, and taught me to never give up; for never hesitating to take Will, from the first hospital visit and years that followed, so I could fight for Oren…whose feet are finally back leaving footprints on our path. I am grateful that final edits to incomplete stories do not apply only to my words.

For Will, who has endured the years as the big brother of a special needs sibling, for all the help, and lessons he taught me.

For Leroy, my husband, best friend, and the other part of my soul, for where we are on our continued journey, despite distance and circumstance.

Printed in the United States
By Bookmasters